Starting and Staying

A guide to opening and sustaining a successful beauty business

ADRIAN TABB

Copyright © 2023 by Adrian Tabb

All rights reserved. No part of this book may be used or reproduced by any means, graphic, electronic, or mechanical, including photocopying, recording, taping, or by any information storage retrieval system, without the written permission of the publisher except in the case of brief quotations embodied in critical articles and reviews.

Published By: Janay Roberson
Awaken U Publishing
www.janayroberson.com

ISBN: 979-8-9870624-5-6

Printed in the United States of America

Table of Contents

Introduction 1

Chapter 1 – Know Who You Are As A Service Provider! 3

Chapter 2 – Be Honest About Your Strengths 7

Chapter 3 – Don't Be Deceived! 11

Chapter 4 – Advertising 15

Chapter 5 – Consultation, Safety Guidelines, Release Forms . 29

Chapter 6 – Deposits, Rufunds, and Business Policies 33

Chapter 7 – Boundaries 39

Chapter 8 – Alternate Streams of Income 43

Chapter 9 – Business and Tax Information 63

Chapter 10 – Health 67

Chapter 11 – Accountability 69

Chapter 12 – Encouragement 73

About the Author 75

Introduction

The beauty industry has progressed over the decades, but there are some key things to help you be consistent and successful as a beauty industry professional. This book will discuss some foundational information I have collected over the 19 years I have been in the beauty industry that will help you start and stay in business! Feel free to take these truths and add to them to make sure you have a unique and fruitful journey as an entrepreneur! God Bless!

CHAPTER 1

Know Who You Are As A Service Provider!

The cosmetology industry has various avenues that you can take as you strive to build a successful career. As cosmetologists, barbers, nail technicians, and makeup artists, we must be intentional about studying the targeted area of services that our clients are paying us for. There are so many needs that a client may have, and those needs will require you to become a specialist under the umbrella of the business that you practice. I'll use myself as an example.

My focus in the salon is hair. I offer sewn-weave services. That includes frontals, closures, and traditional installs. I also offer quickweave services, haircutting, hair coloring, wig creation, and braiding. However, I specialize in sewn weaves and pixie cuts. I know this, and I use this information to my business's advantage. My specialties are what have predominantly shaped how I serve, create, and modify my business for my clientele. Now that my specialties are identified in my career, I can effortlessly draw the clientele that matches my strengths.

Beginners may not know their strengths yet, so I suggest to you beginners in the industry: turn down as little money as possible. You must be available. Take as many clients as you can to get the word out about yourself as a stylist. Not to go too far into marketing just yet, but everything about this chapter and the others serve as a marketing tool for you to recruit your clients. Building a clientele is essential!

It's a crucial time in your career. In fact, It will set the tone for how people view your customer service skills and it will help people determine if they want to continue to support your business. Again, availability is crucial, especially as a beginner. You may be amazingly talented, but as a new face, you're a risk-factor in the eyes of those who haven't been serviced by you yet. People are wondering, upon giving your services a try, will you listen to their instructions and comprehend it enough to execute the job right. Will you be friendly? Will you be timely? Will you be affordable? The more available you are, the quicker you get your feet wet, and the more experience you get under your belt to mold your schedule and your skills to what your clients both need and desire. Understanding your specialties is great, but you also have to make sure you have consistent business to apply your skills to. No availability quickly equates to having no clients, no money, and a dying business. There's always someone doing what you're doing; people move on quickly. Remember that!

CHAPTER 2

Be Honest About Your Strengths

Remember that I already disclosed my business strengths to you, but what about weaknesses? Everyone has them, no matter how good they are. I'll put myself on "front street" again: I offer some coloring services, but COLORING IS NOT MY STRENGTH!!! (I've failed at it on several occasions) Since I know this weakness, I've taken classes to perfect the few color services that I do now offer. Furthermore, I'm honest with my clients and potential clients about their color needs.

Why am I sharing this? You must have a plan for your weaknesses. Honesty is also showing integrity. Don't be quick to book a client for work that you know you haven't studied, practiced and don't feel confident about doing just for money. That behavior will close doors for you quicker than the ones that are opening. One bad move gets people talking. And like gossip, society can both see and hear what you're doing right and wrong in your customer service from witnesses (your clients).

I have friends in the cosmetology arena that I will refer clients to for color. Although I will miss out on a little money here and there, this is why I rely on my specialties to make money for me. I'm able to charge premium rates for these services because of my skill level. Sharing the wealth with my industry friends keeps the door open for networking and comradery.

Clients may pull on you for certain services they really want you to provide, but you may not be the most proficient provider of those styles at your present skill level. This is where you take the time to practice your craft, especially if it's a service you'd like to eventually make your specialty. Find a few people who will allow you to practice (they're out there) and perfect your service. You can offer the clients the services you are practicing for free or at a discounted price. Once you really master the technique you were practicing, you can then offer this newly developed service to clients at an introductory rate. This will give you more practice and you will not miss out on money. Once performing this service becomes second nature, you can charge what it's worth and not just receive the introductory rate.

Being honest with yourself is the most important part in understanding your strengths and weaknesses. Honesty is also how you maintain your strengths and improve your weaknesses. It's ok to request help or take a class! Never allow yourself to become intimidated by the industry, industry professionals or clients. If you struggle completing a style or notice that your work doesn't look like the work of a fellow industry professional who is proficient, seek help in virtual tutorials, classes, and or other stylists. Show yourself friendly. There are some stylists out there who are eager to help you improve. They may have too much clientele, and once they help you, they'll be able to send some your way. Think optimistically in this industry.

CHAPTER 3

Don't Be Deceived!

The hair industry caters to the mere desires of the client, while overlooking the needs. We are in a world where image is everything and people are driven by platforms and possessions. And I have seen so many people intimidated and confused based on social media posts.

Understand that techniques are different for each stylist and client. There have been several claims that "if a style isn't done like this, it's not right". That may be okay for THAT client. But you have to assess the needs for your client. For example, four bundles of hair may be too much for a client experiencing hair loss. You have to determine that, not the stylist on social media.

There are other "suggestions" made by social media influencers that may be detrimental for your clients. You must perform a client consultation and really take into consideration what will work when it comes to chemicals like glue, color, relaxer, etc. In other words, DON'T ALLOW YOURSELF TO BE BULLIED! Think things through and be logical! Assess each situation to determine the best outcome.

Social media is just like the areas around the checkout counters at stores. The contents or products are there to get you to impulsively purchase. It's a strategy to get sales (or followers). We have to separate the need and intent from impulse when using social media.

There have been many images that portray riches and wealth and that can happen! But that should not be the focus of your career. Set goals but be realistic and understand that your path to get to your goals may look a lot different than others. Always remember that social media is used to advertise and advertisement plays with your emotions. Let your journey be professional and not emotional. Remember some are paid to use certain products or wear certain clothing on social media. They can trick you into believing that their lives are matching what they are selling! To some it's just about the dollar at that moment. Build a business that is focused on reality and not an image or a paid promotional transaction

CHAPTER 4

Advertising

Advertising is a major key in the success of your business. It is the billboard that introduces and promotes you and the services you offer. There are a lot of people who will skip traditional advertising and miss several leads on making money because only one form of advertising is preferred over others.

Business Cards

Business Cards are frowned upon now because of Facebook and Instagram. But they are still effective! Business cards work well for your clients who are not on social media. They also are great for those who can't use phones at work but can easily hand a potential customer a card. Cards are present and visible so they are easy reminders for someone to call or view your social media to research your services. They are great to have for events as well. No matter what you are told, business cards will ALWAYS be necessary.

Flyers

Flyers are just as necessary as business cards and are good to have for events as well. They are great to place at beauty supply stores, Laundry facilities, apartment leasing offices, and other businesses who will allow you to promote your work. Flyers are a great way for you to show pictures of your work and give more details about what your business offers. Be careful to not put too much information on the flyer. You don't want it to be overwhelming for the viewer. A flyer should also point people to your website or social media to learn more about you. The flyer should introduce you but not have so much information that the viewer neglects further study of who you are and what you have to offer.

Social Media Promotion

Social media provides platforms for free and paid promotion. It's great to use for people of all ages by providing information at the customer's fingertips on their phones and tablets. You can always be visible and accessible for questions via social media.

Facebook

Facebook advertising offers so many opportunities. A simple post featuring your work is effective in showcasing what you offer. Going a step further by providing a description or a hair tip about the picture will show people how knowledgeable you are. Some customers prefer the knowledge and haircare over a hairstyle. You will gain more clients of substance this way. They will be more consistent in coming when they know they are dealing with a hair care professional and not just someone who can create a look.

You can also utilize the Facebook Live option to advertise as well. Live question and answer sessions will help tell people who you are and help them decide if you are the perfect stylist for them. Working on a model/client on Facebook Live will allow the people to see your skill and technique as will. This is a way to attract the customer with your abilities.

If you have a Facebook business page (highly suggested), you can use it to post the same kinds of hair posts you have on your personal page. You can have a Facebook Live experience on the business page as well. Most importantly, you can post business hours and other helpful information there. There is also a feature that lets you pay for promotion. You can either pay to promote the page or a specific post. This feature allows you to select the audience you'd like to target. Paid promotions are great to generate new followers, content shares, and post engagement. Do not feel embarrassed or desperate about purchasing ads. Think of Facebook as a big newspaper that everyone reads. Just like you'd purchase an ad in a paper, you can for Facebook!

Instagram

Instagram targets a younger audience and allows you to share pictures and videos with captions and hashtags. Hashtags are key because they are used to search different content. For example, I use the search feature on Instagram to find a barber if I'm out of town and need a haircut. I am able to see his or her work and business information just by searching "ATLBARBER" or "atlantamobilebarber".

Be creative with hashtags but also use hashtags that are popular or common. The more you use the hashtags, the more people are able to see your work and would be likely to follow you or use your services. I personally use my name as a hashtag, the name of the salon, my specialties, etc. Whatever category I want to be associated with, I turn into a hashtag.

You can also utilize the Instagram Live feature, which just like Facebook, will give you the opportunity to interact with clients and potential clients. It's a great tool to share and communicate with more people in the beauty industry.

Paid promotions are available if you have a business account on Instagram and you can also pay others for promotion on their accounts. THESE PROMOTIONS WORK!!! I have acquired followers and business from these promotions and developed great relationships with other industry professionals. Invest in promotions frequently.

Another tip to remember with Facebook and Instagram is to always post new content! People want to see your consistency. A lot of times if you are out of sight, you are out of mind. Don't lose traction by not having content. Schedule regular photo shoots and take pictures of your work often!! Consumers love videos. Post as many as you can, but "flooding" timelines with content can have an adverse reaction. Use moderation while remembering to be consistent.

Website/Booking Site

Having a website is going to help generate a lot of income for your business. It will provide an online presence for people to learn more about you and will also show up in some web searches when people are NOT looking for you! Your business card and flyers should always direct people to your website.

Your website should include history (an "about" page) discussing your business, pictures, contact information, and products. Having the products available on the website will generate extra income as well as advertise your professionalism and all the aspects of your company. The website should be designed with your personality and all you want to convey being considered. A well put together site, whether it's for booking or ecommerce, will gain a person's interest almost immediately!

Word of Mouth

This form of FREE advertising will allow your customers to give testimonials to any potential clients. When customers are complimented on their hair or nails, it boosts their self-esteem thus providing a moment for them to give you, the professional, the best review! Remember to provide the best experience for your customers because this is where the review will begin. Potential clients love great reviews.

Although word of mouth could be one of your biggest forms of advertisement, getting people to share who you are and what you do isn't always easy. There are some clients who will be slow to share with some people due to fear of you becoming too busy for them. You want to assure them that you are available for them as well as new clients. I explain that if they tell others about me, it keeps prices lower! LOL! Help me, help you!

Referral Programs, Discounts, and Memberships

Referral Programs

In addition to advertising by word of mouth you can add referral programs to give the customer an incentive to share your information with potential customers. This incentive should give the current customer a discount or free service based on how many potential customers actually come to the salon for services. This is a great way to get the customer motivated to share information especially if the customer is a weekly customer or a customer who gets costly services.

Discounts

Discounts are great to offer to potential customers to get them in your chair for the first time. This gives them the opportunity to get acquainted with your services especially if they feel that what you offer is more costly than they would like to pay. Once they see that your services and knowledge are worth what you charge, they will come back. The discount was just a tool for you to give your best to obtain a lifelong customer.

Oftentimes we are hesitant about offering discounts, but discounts can really motivate customers to return or even get more services. A small discount won't hurt as long as you don't make it a habit and always explain to the customer that this is a one-time event. Make sure the customer knows what the regular price is at that moment so there will be no confusion during the next appointment. If you are keeping client profiles (I suggest you do), document the discount and the full price in the file.

The use of referral cards and coupons will really help with referral programs and discounts. Discount card or coupons are great to offer clients as an incentive for repeat visits. You can offer a free service after so many visits or you can have cards that offer a percentage off a client's first service. These are good for the client who loves a deal, even if it's $5 off. There are so many people who have gone to digital marketing only and that's ok for a certain group of people. But there are people who still like cards, manual booking, and paper trails. (One of those people is ME lol).

There are older customers who may have mastered making a call on a cell phone, buy may not have the patience or understanding for online booking. Some may not know how to send your Facebook page, Instagram, or website to a friend to see your work. There may be coworkers who want to share your info in passing. The quickest way may be to hand them a business card or a referral card. The referral card should have clear information about the regular customer's discount and the potential customer's discount. This could easily be $5 off or 10% off the total service. You may even offer a specific service for free. Keep in mind that whatever you offer as a discount must not take too much away from what you would want to make from the service. We never want to offer 50% off the total service (unless you are feeling extremely generous that day) but we want to entice the customer to book, show our skills, and get them on the book REGULARLY. If you are known as the professional who always gives discounts, no one will book with you until you are offering a "special"!

Membership Programs

Another way to keep customers coming back is to offer membership programs. Have the customer pay a set fee each month for the basic services they will always want to receive. This works especially well for weekly customers. Calculate the cost of what the customer will need each week (or bi-weekly) and offer a discounted rate for their Membership package. This may encourage those who are bi-weekly customers to schedule weekly. If so, just adjust the membership package. You'll find that your clients who are on fixed incomes will love this plan and will encourage others to schedule with you for services. Remember, if the customer feels that you are taking care of them, they will return the favor and take care of you!

CHAPTER 5

Consultation, Safety Guidelines, Release Forms

There should always be a consultation done with each customer. We have all learned the importance of the initial meeting and conversation with a customer. But due to the fact that some are busy or don't see the need to have a consultation, it's become a practice that is almost nonexistent!

I strongly encourage consultation forms! Have the potential customer fill one out and use it to discuss information. Be sure to ask about allergies and medications. Also ask about preferences they may have. Share insight on why this consultation is needed. Typically, customers will be astounded by your level of professionalism and feel that they are in a safer business with a qualified professional.

There are several situations that can be avoided as a result of performing the consultation. I've encountered clients who are allergic to wheat. And because wheat is a common ingredient in relaxers, we had to stick with one particular brand. There was only one brand that would not give her a reaction! Had we not discussed this, there could have been irritation of her scalp, sores, blisters, or even hair loss. But a simple conversation avoided this.

If you are a braider, ask about nickel allergies. There is nickel in some braiding hair and it can induce hair loss if the client already suffers from hair loss issues.

If you are a barber and you are performing color services, be sure to ask about color allergies, particularly henna. Do not just apply color and not think to consult. Chemicals can do a lot of scarring and damage. We want to maintain integrity and the ability to still use our skills in the industry.

Avoid a lawsuit and perform a consultation!!!

Release Forms

Since there are so many issues that can arise from chemical reactions we want to take our precautions to another level by also having the customer sign release forms before services.

Customers don't always know their allergies and some are not going to be honest about having allergies. For this reason always have a release form for chemical and extension services to cover you in the event that a reaction to any product you use occurs.

It's not a bad idea to have them sign for ALL services. A client may be allergic to an ingredient in shampoo or conditioner as well. These seem like extreme measures, but they will protect you in the long run from attacks on your character, professionalism, business, and practices. You can use release forms from your insurance companies, or create your own. Just make sure it releases you from all liability in case of allergic reaction and/or improper removal of extensions.

Safety Guidelines

Your safety guidelines need to be posted on your wall. Since we are now dealing with a global pandemic and everyone has different beliefs about how the pandemic should be handled, posting information visibly will set the tone for your business and the requirements for your area. These are not up for debate. Stand firm on your convictions because your business will have multiple visitors and you want to keep everyone as safe as possible. Remember, it's YOUR business and you have the right to enforce the policies that make your business succeed.

CHAPTER 6

Deposits, Rufunds, and Business Policies

Deposits

The beauty and barber industry makes money based on how well we manage time. Because of this, extra precaution must be taken when booking customers. Non-refundable deposits are a great way to safeguard your time and money.

New customers are often searching for the best option for their needs and even when they book with you they are still searching. That is their right and you can't take that from them. But when they schedule with you and don't show up or cancel in advance.. That's a problem!!

Many times you have turned others away because you have scheduled a new customer, but when they don't show you've missed their money and the money of the potential customer you had to turn away because you were booked already. For this reason a non-refundable deposit is suggested. This holds the booking customer accountable for the time they selected and makes them more cautious about skipping the scheduled time. This way even if they don't show, you have still received money for the time you set aside for the customer. Now if you make wigs, man units, or press-on nails, you can use this time to work on selling products or increasing your visibility on social media. It's a win/win situation for you this way!

Another thing to remember is the more costly a service, the better it is to charge a deposit. This is whether the customer is new or not. My practice in the salon is to charge a 50% deposit for any service totalling $100 or more. So if a service total is $200, the deposit is $100.

The deposit payment is sometimes over 50% of the total cost If the customer is ordering extensions. The cost of a sewn weave in my salon is $200. So if a customer orders extensions from me for the service and the total for the extensions alone is $300, the $300 must be paid in advance for the service. I do this to ensure that the cost of the extensions is secured and if the customer cancels the appointment, they can still come by and pick up the hair and I already secured my profit from the sale.

Refunds

It's important that we remember that the time it takes us to do the work we do is what generates our pay. Because of this, I don't offer refunds on services. Once a service is done and the requested look has been executed, payment must be received!!!

Sometimes a customer isn't happy and honestly that isn't our fault (unless the style is poorly executed). We must be honest in this situation and put pride aside to determine if it's your fault because of poor execution or if the customer just made a mistake in choice of style. Also don't fall victim to the "I love it when I'm in the salon but when I got home my boyfriend hated it" customer. That's a boyfriend/girlfriend issue, not a stylist/customer issue. In cases like this I will offer alternative methods to resolve issues a customer may have with her hair. Such as a new style at a discounted rate, but never a refund.

Business Policies

With the mention of refunds, it's important to say that policies about refunds and other important salon information should be visibly posted in the salon. Posting the information about your refund policy will show that you are being fair with everyone and no one can say you made up a rule just because of the situation you may have with them.

You want to list things in your policies like rules for bringing children, booking and rebooking policies, showing up late for an appointment, and requirements for guests coming to the salon.

Your rules and wishes should be addressed and listed so there is no confusion on what is requested for each person who comes to the salon. If you have a website or booking site, your policies should be listed there as well. New customers will be aware of the rules before coming to the salon.

Price List

Price List used to be the biggest post on the salon walls and we all used to be fascinated with reading them! I suggest that along with your policies you post your prices as well. Even if it's in the form of a brochure, prices need to be visible to the public to ensure that no one is left in the dark as to what needs to be paid. Total costs should be mentioned in the consultation, but prices also need to be on the wall or in a brochure so everyone feels like the prices that are listed are for everyone and are fair. Many people ask about the cost of the services and want to share the information with others. Brochures offer that information. (along with cards that list the website as a resource to see policies and prices).

CHAPTER 7

Boundaries

Working as a professional in the beauty and barber industry, you will encounter several people and they are not all the same. While you will need to know them well to help provide assistance with their needs as a customer, you must set clear and consistent rules and boundaries.

Most customers like to relax and unwind when they come to the salon. That is totally understood and expected in most cases. We hear everything from babydaddy/babymama drama, to family messiness, to work issues and problems with the kids. Customers feel free to share these personal moments with us and expect not to hear what they share from another source after leaving your establishment.

Over the years I made the terrible mistake of revealing some of my life's most intimate details. I learned quickly that even though it was entertaining and made the time go by fast, it wasn't the right thing to do. Don't get me wrong, sharing family vacations and light details is fine. Drama in your relationships or business affairs is not up for discussion. I've even been a customer who had to listen to someone's rants and it was the most uncomfortable situation. Meditate, pray, call your bestie! But do NOT bring your customers into your situations. It's unprofessional and does not make them closer to you! It pushes them further away and you can lose a customer quickly. Understand that the business must go on in spite of what you are going through and if you are that distraught, take a break and reschedule your customers. They deserve the best your skill has to offer.

Also when listening to your customer, be wise to know what is your concern and what is not. Some things will require you to pray for them in silence. Some things will require you to physically do nothing. And some things may warrant giving a little advice. But never make their burden yours. Disconnect from the mentality that you must save everyone. Some things are not your assignment and that's okay!!! You are not doing them a disservice if you don't have an answer to their needs. You are however doing yourself a disservice if you continue to extend yourself beyond what you are purposed to do. Boundaries are healthy for you to maintain your sanity and for you not to confuse the customer any more than they may already be.

CHAPTER 8

Alternate Streams of Income

As a beauty enhancer, you will go through ups and downs of customers and retention. Some customers will decide to move, get braids, some will decide to seek services from someone else, others will have emergencies and won't be able to come in for their appointments. There will also be times you experience overloads in appointments. These will include income tax season, Easter, Mothers Day, Proms, Graduations, Christmas, etc. Prepare to offer the best services during these times because your time and energy will be stretched thin! But prepare for the times you will experience the loss of customers, too. During these moments you will need to focus on the other streams of income you can offer.

Retail Products

Selling products to your clients is a great way to make more money in the salon. It actually builds your customers trust in you because you are sharing your recommendations or what you actually use on their hair in the salon. Don't be afraid to sell them what you use. The fact that they will know what's being used on the hair is a plus! This makes your job easier.

You can get discounted rates by buying in bulk from some distributors or you can purchase from your local professional beauty supply stores. You can also contact different product companies and order directly from them. Your retail (mark up price for the customer) should ensure that you receive a profit for the sale. Remain stocked because some people will come in just for the products and not receive a service. This can ensure a large amount of revenue.

Have a variety of products and consider what the customers' husbands, wives, and children may need. Have something stocked for each person in the family.

Retail can be taken a step further by creating your own line of products by either using the private label option or custom formulation. Private labeling is using a product or series of products that a company already has created and you sell it under your brand using your name. This is extremely common. You may be familiar with a company and like the shampoo or gel that the company sells. Contact them and ask if they are willing to create a private label agreement with you and move forward with purchasing in bulk, get the ingredient list, print labels, get safety data sheets made, and sell your products!!!

There are companies that are private label specific. They only exist to sell to those what want to have their own brands. Contact those companies, research and test the products, and follow the steps mentioned above to make your own line of products. This option is especially important if you are also an educator and you travel to trade shows. You will need something to put in the hand of the student/consumer to remember you by and something to sell to offset the cost of traveling to participate in the trade shows. Retail is a great way to make money and promote your brand. This advertisement will forever make an impression and keep people wanting more!

To accompany the products, you may also sell scarves, satin caps, combs, brushes, and pillowcases. Scarves, satin caps, and satin pillowcases are great items to sell to protect the customers investment for their services. Oftentimes customers don't have enough of them or have lost them, or simply don't understand the importance of having them. Be sure to educate them and offer the products for purchase. You may find them from wholesale companies or at trade shows for a great price or you may purchase at beauty supply stores and mark up the prices to retail. A personalized touch through a wholesale company is also great to have something else with your brand represented.

Combs and brushes are great to sell your brand as well. Have some made with your logo and sell them or even give them away in some cases for brand awareness. You would be surprised at how many customers don't have those items! Plus if they need new ones, it's more convenient for them to purchase from you instead of heading to a supply store.

Selling virgin hair, closures, frontals, and premade wigs from overseas vendors will always be an important means of making money. Whether you install wigs and hair or not, you can make a great profit on those products. I don't advertise that I sell hair to the general public, but I do market to my current and new customers. I initially decided to sell extensions because I was overwhelmed by the amount of people who would bring me hair that was terrible. I could at least sell the hair I knew was great or if I got a bad batch of hair I could speak with my vendors to get replacement hair.

When deciding to sell extensions, you will need to do a lot of research to see what vendor's hair will work for you. Take your time and build relationships with them! This will be vital when doing continued business with them. Assess how much hair you can order at once when you determine the vendor with great quality and pricing. The more you buy at one time, the better deal you get on pricing per bundle and the better deal you get on shipping costs. This will be best because you won't spend so much on shipping that it takes away from the potential profit.

Pricing of the wigs, bundles, frontals, and closures should be based on how much you are paying in wholesale costs. For example, if a bundle costs me $40 before shipping costs, I will retail that bundle for $75 in the salon. If a wig costs me $89, I will retail it for $130 and up. Your profit depends on YOU! You can sell those items at a lower or higher rate. You have to determine what works for your business and your customers. Just be mindful that you want a business that lasts. Don't price the product so low that there is no profit or means of purchasing new inventory.

Be sure to sell what's popular in your area. If people like curly hair where you live, keep it stocked or promote it heavily! If people wear more straight hair, make it your product of choice. You must do a lot of research to see what is needed in your city or state and you may want to explore the option of online sales as well. This would be big for your extension business because you would have the ability to reach so many others with your products.

If you are interested in wig (unit) making, you could also add them to your service menu along with the maintenance and install of the units. Wig creation has made me a significant amount of money over the years of my career. I go to supply stores and look for stores online that have discounted, but good quality remy or yaky hair to make wigs with and then sell them. Many times I find the hair that we used to purchase for $50 to $100 for $3 up to $20 dollars. That's a deal I can't pass up!!!

Because most people are purchasing virgin hair, stores are doing all they can to get rid of remy and yaky hair from their inventories. Take advantage of this to purchase as much hair as you can to sell to customers and to make wigs with.

I can typically make a unit by hand in 30 to 40 minutes. So imagine the money that can be made by charging $150-$300+ for a unit that took you all of 40 minutes to make! This is an example of working smart and not hard. You can also make a bigger profit if you use virgin hair to make the units. Either virgin, yaky, or remy hair units can last for years with proper maintenance and care. I have customers who have had my units for about 11 years now. All it takes for some customers is to get one unit and be hooked on the convenience! Now I have regular clients who also have 8 to 10 of my wigs at home in their wig rooms or closets. People will always buy units for last minute events and/or special occasions. So try to keep them on hand as much as possible to make quick sales. Utilize the time that you have between customers or the time created from "no show" customers to create your units. Having a social media sale will also generate more likes, shares, reposts, and followers for your brand. Soon you will have people requesting to have units made at your regular price.

Art Gallery

Another amazingly creative way to generate money in the salon is to have your salon serve as an art gallery as well. Collaborate with artists to use their art in your establishment and sell them. As one is sold, it is replaced by a new work of art. This way you get to decorate your salon, support local artists, help expose local artists, and make a profit in the process!! I have been doing this for over a year now and it really makes great conversation and great sales. You never know who is needing a work of art for their home or business. Some people will even give them as gifts. As long as you provide the art, you can make a sale.

Non Surgical Hair Replacement

Hair Replacement is another way to generate more income. You can actually build an entire business around hair replacement.

A lot of people are confused initially about this service. People automatically think about surgical hair replacement which involves skin grafts, but I'm referring to non surgical hair replacement. Non

Surgical hair replacement involves the attachment of hair pieces (specific shapes for needed areas) or medical wigs to the clients scalp for a temporary illusion of the existence of natural hair growth. This is done with medical grade adhesives which are stronger than the glues we normally use on wigs for basic salon services.

This service is typically given to those who have hair loss due to medical reasons such as alopecia, hair loss due to medication, the diagnosis of a condition with a side effect of hair loss, cancer treatment patients, and burn survivors. You can bill the customers medical insurance for these services. The cost for a service like this typically starts at $1500 and it's best to work with these customers one-on-one in privacy due to the sensitivity of their conditions. Always begin with a consultation to explain costs and the entire process because this is still not a common service to most in certain areas. Be very clear about maintenance and costs so there are no surprises or confusion in the process of helping your customer.

This service will solve problems for many and you can easily make money in the process by simply dedicating one day a week to offer the service. You could even service customers who need these services on a full time basis. I recommend that you know all the details of the business to make the best transition to the hair loss business. This will include knowing what insurance companies will pay, how much they will pay, will you be in network, and how you will have the person pay the copay. All of that may sound foreign, but it will make a lot of sense if you decide to enter that aspect of service for the customers.

DVDs/Digital Streaming

Beauty industry professionals have always made videos demonstrating how to execute certain styles and techniques. These videos have been an accompaniment when teaching classes. It gives the learner something to take home for further study. These videos can cost just as much as class! I always tell stylists to have at least one to make money on when teaching somewhere. I now have filmed over twenty videos and I've sold them in DVD format on my website, at tradeshows, and classes. I have determined the content of the videos by the popularity of services I provide and the techniques that I know some struggle with. The income has been great especially when the pandemic was first introduced. People bought them to watch while at home and study.

Although DVD format is still good, most people are looking to digitally stream. You will make a great deal of supplemental income this way as well but you must record your videos in the correct format for the digital platform you want to use. This will require a bit of research to execute well.

Classes

Hosting classes based on the skills that you're strong in will create an amazing flow of income. Having knowledge of what you are strong in helps you capitalize on the talent. For example, I'm strong with 27 piece extensions and all phases of short hairstyling. I can host several classes throughout the year demonstrating different looks, techniques, and product knowledge. You can have group classes and/or offer one on one sessions. Think about it! 50 students paying at least $50 per class, is a total of $2,500 on attendance alone. You can price the tickets even higher. Also if you sell retail, you'll make money on the products as well. If you sell DVD'S or digital streams of your beauty demonstrations, you will make money from those the day of the class as well.

If you want to focus on one on one classes you can start pricing them over $100 and sell products and DVD's as well. You can provide an intimate space for the learner to absorb all you have to offer. You can provide a variety of classes and have them listed on your website for people to read about, pay in advance, and schedule the session! This is a win for you and the learner! Ease of payment, Secured Income!

You can also start hosting classes for others or hosting classes and paying stylists to come in to teach. You can host classes for others and get paid by the stylist to put the class together and get a percentage of the sales. This is a great way to make money without actually having to teach as well. Use the gift you possess to organize and structure and get paid. If you decide to bring an artist or guest stylist in, you can pay them a flat fee and take the sales at the door. Everyone will win and get exposure.

When planning a class please remember to factor in expenses such as the venue, sound equipment, refreshments, promotional materials, travel, and other expenses when deciding on a price for the attendees. You want an affordable class for them, but it has to make financial sense for you as well.

Education

Just as I mentioned that you can make money from hosting classes, it's just as important that you realize you need to attend them as well. Education is always ongoing in what we do as industry professionals. You can always learn something to make you better or make your time work better for you. It's true that when you know better, you should do better!

Product knowledge classes are important because knowing what a product is formulated for and what the ingredients are will give you a lot of insight as to how to use the product. So many times I've heard people say products don't work. What I've found out is that most people don't read about how to actually use the product so they over or under use the product. Getting the information from the company or seeing someone use the product while giving the explanation is crucial.

Actually, attending product knowledge classes will help you understand how to use the products and get helpful tips on how to use the product in other ways. For example, you may be using the product as a curl wax and it may be able to be used to aid in eyebrow shaping or dry molding. There are so many options when using certain products that you may actually save tons of money by using one product for multiple uses.

Having information on the ingredients is important for consultation purposes. Knowing what makes up a product will help you during consultations determine if a client is allergic to anything in the product. Knowing this will save you time and money when deciding what to use for each client.

Knowing the ingredients will also help you explain to the customer what you are using and why. This information may help you make your tip! The customer will appreciate the information you have to share with them and know that you are well versed in your craft. This may seem small but customers like to know that you take pride in learning about your industry.

Styling Techniques

I often tell people when I teach classes that I can not teach them style but I can teach them techniques. If you can learn techniques, you will always be able to create styles. Attending classes that display techniques is crucial when trying to learn new trends. Product knowledge is good to know, as technique and product usage work together. There are repetitive concepts that help to build certain looks and learning these concepts can enhance your speed, neatness, and accuracy in accomplishing the goal of styling. Never think that you have it all figured out when it comes to your technical strengths. You will always find that there is something that will help you be better. It may be simple but it may change the way you style hair completely!

CHAPTER 9

Business and Tax Information

Many stylists joined the industry because of the love of the craft, but many have neglected the business aspect of what we do. Most of the time our businesses are not respected because of our lack of business preparation and planning. During the beginning of the Covid pandemic, many beauty industry professionals didn't qualify for financial assistance because business licenses had not been obtained and other paperwork was not readily available. From accounting, to taxes, to licenses, to certifications, there's always work that has to be done to run a legitimate business. Always seek professional business advice. Attending classes about business is good to obtain general knowledge and make contacts that can help you along the way. You will find these classes available at trade shows and local seminars.

Here are some key things to remember:

1. Make sure that you have a business license with the city your business is located in.

2. Make sure your business is incorporated. (Consult with a professional to determine if an LLC, Scorp, or another entity is best for you)

3. Always make sure you research the necessary licenses and/or certifications for the services you want to offer.

4. Have a business bank account.

5. Find out how to increase business credit (Duns, credit card, etc.)

BUSINESS AND TAX INFORMATION

6. Make sure the physical location you want to lease for your business is zoned properly with the city to house the business you want to open (residential vs commercial and can a beauty business be opened at the address).

7. Determine how you will keep track of expenses, income, tax payments, and yearly expenses.

8. Learn all you can about tax laws and try to work with the same professional yearly for your taxes. Hiring a CPA is strongly suggested.

Although these things may seem tedious, they are necessary and will help you build a business that will not only make you happy, but you will build a business that will continue to grow.

CHAPTER 10

Health

Education about health may seem like the furthest thing from your mind, especially since the information you've been reading has been about beauty and business. Health is just as important to running a successful business. You have to be good to yourself before you can be good to others. So you must take time to eat properly, get rest, visit the doctor regularly, exercise, and be stress-free!

I've learned the hard way. Poor diet and exercise have sent me on quite the journey of physical health and even complications. I've learned the importance and I don't hesitate to now share that it's important to be conscious of your body and all it needs to survive. Everyone has different needs, but please have your blood sugar and blood pressure checked often. Also, make sure you drink plenty of water!!

Read and ask your doctor questions. If you're not getting the help you need, search for another doctor and do health research yourself. Remember, hair health starts on the inside. Be the example for your customers!

CHAPTER 11

Accountability

In this industry you will always need direction. This may be in business, skill enhancement, or help opening different avenues of services. Being accountable for your business goes without stress, but being accountable to someone for your business could be the answer to many of your business needs. Here are a couple ways to have accountability: Shadowing and Mentorship

Shadowing

Shadowing is typically done when you are monitoring a professional's day to day operations in a salon, focusing on either technical abilities or professionalism. I like to look at shadowing as on the job training and most of the time the professional you shadow makes sure you master the skill you are looking to learn. Some slow down the daily functions to ensure you get it or will check on you at some point to make sure you are well on your way to nailing the skill.

All professionals are not open to this option, because they fear losing business to the one they are training. Be sure to research and not be anxious when looking for someone to shadow. Accountability with the right professional will be easy because there will be a willingness to share and a desire to see you win!

Mentorship

Mentorship often allows one a closer, more intimate journey with a professional when it comes to business accountability. Mentors often offer resources and personal information on how to make your business thrive not just in technical ability but in business stability. Most mentorship is not done in the salon but in meetings and telephone sessions. Some mentors will charge you for the information and that may be best for you. When you pay for information, you're more likely to utilize it. Research and ask questions before making the final decision on selecting a mentor. In your search, be mindful that the mentorship is not hired to be your friend, but to make you better in the realm of business. You are supposed to learn not find the person who wants to hang out and have fun. You owe it to your customers and business reputation to make your business practices a priority.

CHAPTER 12

Encouragement

I could not write this book and not encourage you! This is not always going to be the most glamourous journey but it will be rewarding knowing you did what you were created to do. This is just the beginning for some of you and the bit of information that some of you needed to make it to the next level of business. No matter where you are right now, there is no need to feel discouraged or no need to run from the future. You are equipped with everything you need to accomplish the task set before you. Believe in yourself and give yourself the opportunity to grow. Have Faith! Pray! Meditate!

Take Breaks! But don't you dare start to doubt your purpose! You have been created to do this! It doesn't matter how many are already in the business or how many have intimidated you in the past. They don't have the same vision as you and won't change the lives you've been called to. THEY WILL NEVER BE YOU!!!!!!! So confidently walk in your destiny and make every effort to grow and be the answer that you, your family, your friends, and your tribe will need. Your steps are ordered! Nothing happens without a reason! I'm expecting great things from you!!

Be Great!
Adrian T.

About the Author

Adrian began his professional journey at the age of 18 at Arthur's Beauty College in Pine Bluff, AR. After becoming licensed as a cosmetologist in Arkansas, he also went on to get licensed in Texas and Georgia. He is a licensed cosmetology instructor in Georgia and Arkansas. He has also served as a member of the CTAC for the Arkansas State Board of Cosmetology.

Adrian owns AMT Salon and Hair Replacement Center, LLC. where he offers services for clients, Instructional Videos, and One-on-One and Group training.

Adrian travels throughout the year to various hair shows and seminars to educate and share with other industry professionals.

Adrian also is the Pastor of Kingdom Builders Ministries in Holly Grove, AR. His passion for ministry is just as strong as his passion for the hair industry.

Hair and the Integrity of the industry are important to Adrian. He plans to continue this journey one client and one class at a time.

Contact and Booking

If you would like more information or to book Adrian for you conference, seminar, workshop, or podcast, please contact him at adriantabb@yahoo.com

Follow and Support
Facebook: Adrian Tabb
Instagram: @adriantabb
Website: www.adriantabb.net
Clubhouse: Adrian Tabb
TikTok: ariantabb03
LinkedIn: Adrian Tabb

www.ingramcontent.com/pod-product-compliance
Lightning Source LLC
Chambersburg PA
CBHW031638160426
43196CB00006B/469